DO THE RIGHT THING

How to Stay Cool in Any Social Situation

by Roxanne Camron

SCHOLASTIC INC.
New York   Toronto   London
Auckland   Sydney   Mexico City
New Delhi   Hong Kong

ISBN 0-439-16118-5

Copyright © 2000 by Scholastic Inc.
Published by Scholastic Inc., 555 Broadway,
New York, NY 10012.

SCHOLASTIC and associated logos
are trademarks and/or registered
trademarks of Scholastic Inc.

12 11 10 9 8 7 6 5 4 3 2 1
0 1 2 3 4 5/0   01

Printed in the U.S.A.
First Scholastic printing, May 2000

TABLE OF CONTENTS

Intro

Have you ever felt clueless 'cause you just didn't know how to handle a social situation? Maybe you weren't sure what to say to a grown-up, or how to act at a friend's house, or how to introduce your parents to your teacher. Not knowing what's expected of you can make you feel embarrassed and uncomfortable.

What can you do about it? You can get clued in on politeness pointers, manners musts, and etiquette how-tos. Most likely, you already know something about manners and etiquette. Your parents probably taught you your very first manners lesson when you learned to say please and thank you. But manners are a lot more complex than that and are a social skill that everyone needs.

This book is packed with helpful info on all the things you can do to fit in and keep your cool.

Here's what you'll learn:

✳ How to make great first impressions on others.
✳ How to get your friends' parents to like you.
✳ How to feel comfortable in almost any social situation.

✳ How to get along better with your family and
   your pals.
✳ How to get invited places more than once.
✳ How to put others at ease.
✳ How to make better-lasting impressions.

As a result, you'll also feel self-confident. So why
wait? Let's get started.

Chapter 1:

The Rules of Meeting and Greeting

What Would You Do?

You're out shopping with your mom and you bump into a new friend at the mall. You begin chatting and then you realize that your mom and your friend don't know each other. You should:

1. *wait for your mom to introduce herself. Adults are always supposed to make the first move.*

2. *introduce your friend to your mom, saying, "Mom, I'd like you to meet my friend Kelly Turner."*

3. *wait and let your friend introduce herself to your mom.*

The answer: If you chose number 2, you're on your way to mega-manners. It's proper to intro-

3

duce two people who don't know each other, when you know them both. It's also a "manners must" to present the younger person to the adult when introducing them.

One of the times when you'll really get a chance to show off your social savvy is when you're introducing yourself or others. Introductions are in order whenever people don't know each other — and knowing how to handle things just right will come in handy time after time. Some introductions can be casual — like when you're introducing two of your friends. Other intros should be a bit more formal. The cool thing is, the rules of courtesy have changed along with the changing world, so more casual intros are usually considered A-OK. You might be more comfortable using the simplest and least stuffy-sounding introductions — except in formal situations.

Whether you're introducing your friends to your parents, your mom to your teacher, or yourself to a new student at your school, there's some easy-to-learn info that can help you make the right moves no matter who is involved or what the occasion is. And it's really easy to master these manners maneuvers by learning a few helpful how-tos.

First Things First: Introducing Yourself to Others

Making a good first impression starts with what you do, what you say, and how you act. Make sure that when you meet someone for the first time, you smile and look directly at them. If you do, you'll show that you're a friendly, outgoing person. And then chances are they'll want to get to know you.

Sometimes you might find yourself in situations where it's just not practical to stop and wait for a formal introduction. If this happens, don't be shy. It's fine to just walk up to someone you want to meet and say, "Hi, I'm Ann." If there's some other useful bit of information to add, go for it, as in, "We're in the same homeroom."

Introductions Made Easy

Here are some easy guidelines to guarantee you'll make great introductions.

1. When introducing a man to a woman or a guy to a girl, use the woman's name first.

2. When introducing a younger person to an adult, use the adult's name first.

3. When introducing someone in a position of authority (like a minister or teacher) to someone who's not (like your brother), use the VIP's name first.

4. Don't call grown-ups by their first names unless they say it's OK. Continue to call them by Mr., Mrs., Ms., and Miss _____ until they tell you otherwise. *

> Author's note: You'll see this Manners Meltdown symbol throughout the book. It refers to a social situation question you'll be quizzed about at the end of the chapter.

5. When introducing a friend to your parents, give your friend's first and last names. Example: "Mom, I'd like you to meet my friend, Jennifer Lee."

6. Introducing parents or stepparents can sometimes cause confusion since they may have a different last name than yours. If that is the case, you might say, "Ashley, I'd like you to meet my mother and stepfather, Mr. and Mrs.

Owens." Or if your mom uses a different name than your stepfather, you could say, "Ashley, this is my mom, Mrs. Schneider, and my stepdad, Mr. Owens." In this instance, it's perfectly acceptable to use your friend's name first.

7. When introducing two of your friends, you might say, "Erin, this is Lauren. Lauren, meet Erin." But the rules of modern manners also allow for quicker, more informal intros. So, you might just want to say, "Erin, I'd like you to meet Lauren." What if the setting were more formal? In that case, you'd use both first and last names.

8. When you introduce a friend to a small group, say everyone's first name. When you introduce a friend to a large group, just say, "Everybody, this is Kimberly." Then it's everyone's job to chime in and introduce themselves.

Forgetting Names

If your mind goes blank when you're making an introduction, don't say, "I'd like you to meet —

er — a — ugh . . ." Just chill, and admit that you've drawn a blank. Say something like, "Oops, I'm sorry, but I just can't think of your name."

You might say something like this to the person whose name you've forgotten: "Do you know my friend Jocelyn?" Hopefully, the person whose name you can't remember will fill both of you in on her name when she replies. Or you can wait and hope that the two of them will just introduce themselves.

Say What?

When you introduce someone, or when you're being introduced, the words you say can be short, friendly, and direct. Though your mom and dad may prefer that you use formal greetings like, "May I present," or "How do you do?", or "Pleased to meet you," it's often cool to be less formal.

When you are doing the introductions, you may want to say:

"This is . . ."
"Have you met . . . ?"

"Do you know . . . ?"
"I'd like you to meet . . ."

When being introduced, you might want to answer:

"Hi, how are you?"
"Nice to meet you."
Or simply, "Hi."

It's also nice to repeat the name of the person you've just met. Everyone feels good with that personal attention.

No matter what words you use when you're making intros, you'll score points by being pleasant and relaxed — that way everyone else will be, too.

To Shake or Not to Shake

OK, so you've just been introduced to a grown-up and you know what to say, but you're not sure what to do. Here's the scoop.

It's definitely considered proper for a younger person to shake hands with an adult they've just met. But if you feel uncomfortable doing this, you might want to check with your mom or dad ahead of time to see if you've got some leeway. Some families say it's OK to save the shake for formal situations, but you should be prepared for when an adult extends a hand to you first! Here are some helpful grip tips:

A confident handshake will send a message that you're a confident person. Yours shouldn't be clammy, or bone-crushing, or limp. Practice with your mom or dad to make sure your handshake is not too hard — and not too wimpy. Offer your right hand with a firm but gentle squeeze: Your palm should be in the palm of the person you're meeting, your thumb to the side.

✳ Your shake should last about two to three seconds.
✳ Don't offer only your fingertips. Always extend your entire hand.
✳ Smile and look at the person during the handshake.

MANNERS MELTDOWN

"I was riding home with my friend and her mom from a movie, and I wanted to ask her mom a question. I didn't know whether to call her Mrs. Glass or just Susan." — Jeni, age 12

After reading this chapter, would you know what to do in Jeni's situation? If you're not sure, no sweat. Find the **MM*** symbol in this chapter, and you'll find the answer you're looking for.

Chapter 2:

Family Matters

What Would You Do?

You're bummed 'cause you think your parents treat you like a baby. They say they'll start letting you do more when you start acting more mature. You should:

1. *think of a good argument why they should give you more freedom. Be sure to tell them that all of your friends have more privileges than you do.*

2. *uh, forget it for now. They're never gonna lighten up, so why bother saying anything? It'll just lead to a fight.*

3. *be polite and cool-headed, and show respect for their opinions, for them, and for others in your family. You may not get what you want this time, but, hey, you'll be on your way to showing them that you really **are** growing up.*

The answer, natch, is number 3. It's simple. If you want your 'rents to stop treating you like a kid, you need to stop acting like one! The more you show them that you're responsible, the more they'll ease up. Yep. It's true. Try it.

Your family isn't perfect. DUH!!!! All families have their ups and downs, good times and bad, weeks of war and periods of peace. What can you do to make your family life more harmonious? You can make sure you do your part to show respect and consideration for those you care about the most. Here's how to help your fam get along famously.

All in the Family

You probably spend more time with your family than with anyone else you know. So, what better place than at home to practice good manners? Does that mean you have to be on your very best behavior 24/7? No way! But if you get in the habit of being mannerly with the people you love (and live with every day), you'll be off to a great start.

Remember to say please when asking for something and thank you when you get it. It may seem like a little thing, but guess what? It can have a BIG impact on your relationships.

Here are some other tips:

❋ Acknowledge the point of view of others even if you disagree with them. Everyone has an opinion that deserves to be heard — not just you.
❋ Be cheerful. Say hello or good morning to each family member when you first see them.
❋ Talk to your parents. They may want to know more than you want to tell them at times, but it's not polite to cut them off from any and all communication.
❋ Remind yourself that manners are a way to show your family you care about them.

Dealing with Sibs

Sure, it's natural to wish you were an only child sometimes. But it's mucho better to think about how you can get along with your family.

It's not easy for a bunch of people to live under one roof. No matter how hard you try, you're not going to get along all of the time. Why? 'Cause each of you has your own personality — your own special way of doing things. That's why it takes Effort (with a capital E) to ensure domestic tranquillity.

Here are some sibling-survival tips:

* Think about what you usually fight about. Ask yourself, can't we do something better with our time? Figure out what you can do differently to keep the peace.
* Establish some house rules. Ask each other to think of one thing you'd really like the other *not* to do. Maybe your sister will get off the phone when you ask her to, if you promise not to use every last drop of shampoo all the time. Sign a contract to seal the deal.
* Respect each other's privacy. Are you willing to stop borrowing clothes or anything else without asking? Do you swear not to listen in on private conversations? Or eavesdrop on phone calls? Or read notes, yearbook inscriptions, or letters? And how 'bout making sure you knock before entering your sib's room?
* Avoid jealousy. Recognize that each of you has your strong points. Despite what you think, your parents love all of you equally — for your own unique personalities. Don't make comparisons. They probably won't, either.
* Be aware that you won't like each other all of

the time, but you can sure try to GET OVER IT! faster.

* At least some of the time, treat your brothers or sisters like you would close friends.
* Talk to your sibs the way you would talk to your friends' brothers or sisters.
* Learn to say "I'm sorry" when you're wrong.
* Don't run to Mom or Dad with every little thing — or just to make yourself look good.
* Be in a good mood as much as possible. Don't yell, slam doors, or close yourself up in your room.
* Think before you speak. It's hard to take something back once you've blurted it out.
* Do your share of the chores.

The Space Case

If you share a room or a bathroom, sibling relations can really score high on the stress-o-meter. The following tips might help.

Don't make a habit of . . .

. . . throwing your clothes into a heap on the floor. Ditto, leaving your shoes or your backpack out in the middle of the room where someone can trip over them.

. . . rummaging through your sibling's drawers looking for anything you can't find in your own.

. . . staying up way later than your sibling and blasting the TV or CD player.

. . . breaking things that are not yours and not replacing them.

. . . hiding the deodorant or toothpaste, or using all of the hot water.

Shared spaces within your home (like the family room or kitchen) require that you do your share in the consideration department. Don't know where to begin? Here's a good start.

Be sure you . . .

. . . clean up after yourself and take care of your own messes. Don't leave your half-eaten food or dirty plates lying around the kitchen or family room.

. . . don't raid the fridge and eat food that might belong to someone else or that your mom might have intended for dinner. If it doesn't have your name on it, ASK!

. . . don't leave your schoolwork strewn all over the kitchen counter. Clear away any papers you've used, soft-drink cans, and snack-food wrappers.

. . . take turns using the computer, controlling the remote, watching videos, talking on the phone.

If There's Trouble on the Homefront

It's a fact. Parents divorce. Families split up. It's not fun, but it happens. And it doesn't just happen to you. In America, almost one out of every three kids has parents who are divorced. There's not much you can do about it, but there are some things you can do to make the adjustment easier on everyone.

First of all, tell yourself that this has nothing to do with you — and believe it. Instead of spending your time wishing your parents would get back together, think about how you can learn to accept the change your family is going through.

You need to be respectful of your parents' decision. It's never easy for grown-ups to decide to split up. Trust that your parents are breaking up for good reasons. If you aren't sure what they are, you may want to ask your mom and dad to explain things to you.

Here are some other ways to deal:

DO remain loyal to both parents. They love you. You love them. Don't take sides.
DON'T get caught between your parents.
DON'T report one's activities to the other. If they ask you questions about each other or if they're constantly putting each other down, you need to put a stop to it. Tell them you're not comfortable with how they're acting.
DON'T be embarrassed about your situation. Talk with trusted friends about how you're feeling. If you don't feel like talking about it, it's OK to say "I'd rather not discuss this right now."
DO try to put a positive spin on things. Now that your parents aren't fighting, they'll be more fun for you to be around.
DO express your feelings. If you are bummed out about something, say so. Use words like "This is hard for me," or "This really hurts." Saying how you feel will help all of you.
DO realize that your mom and dad will probably date in time. When they do, it's important for you to keep an open mind about

the situation and treat their dates with the same courtesy you would show to any other guest.

Stepfamilies

Most stepfamilies are nothing like Cinderella's. Still, if your family's about to get some new additions, it may be difficult for you to accept. After all, this is a really big change — not just for you, but for everyone.

You need to realize that feeling comfortable (not to mention feeling like a family) is going to take time. At some later point, you may all come to love one another, but right now you're faced with just getting to know each other. It will help to remind yourself that your real mom and dad — and your real brothers and sisters — aren't perfect. So, don't expect your stepfamily to be perfect, either.

Here are some tips to help you on your way to becoming one big, happy family:

Tip #1

Give your new relatives a chance. This isn't exactly easy for them, either. Treat them with courtesy, and allow plenty of time for all of you to get adjusted to this major change. Everyone is likely to be a bit uncomfortable with one another for a while.

Tip #2

Don't ever be rude. If you're feeling frustrated about something, talk it over with your parent. If you think your mom or dad won't listen, talk to an adult friend or a close relative.

Tip #3

Try to be happy for your parent. If you're bummed about being left out, ask your mom or dad to set aside some time to spend one-on-one with you.

Grandparents

Do your grandparents tend to look at the world in their own special way? Maybe they seem a bit old-fashioned. Or maybe they don't seem to understand you and the world you're living in.

Well, sure, that can be challenging to a relationship. But just think of all the good things that they bring into your life, too.

Grandparents have a wealth of knowledge about your family. They can tell you funny and revealing stories about your mom or dad when they were young. And there's probably something your grandma cooks better than anyone — or a game your grandpa's never too busy to play with you.

It's important to treat your grandparents with the respect they deserve. Try to understand that some things may be hard for them to accept because of their values and traditions. Be patient with them. Try asking them about their childhoods, school years, young adult lives, and so on. They have wonderful memories to share with you — and they can give you good advice, too.

Try not to let anything (or everything) your grandparents say embarrass you. Let them know that you're interested in what they have to say, and be sure you show them that you're really listening by asking follow-up questions or by making eye contact when they talk. If they bug you, don't let them know it. Take the time to show them how well-mannered you are, and let your actions demonstrate how much you value, love, and need them.

Chapter 3:

Making Your
Friendships Special

What Would You Do?

You and your friend had a big fight. You thought it would blow over, but now she's acting really rude to you at school. You should:

1. make the first move. Let her know you care enough to try to work things out. Knowing how to talk and listen can strengthen your friendship — and make it even better than before.

2. wait for her to talk to you. She's the one who's still mad.

3. act like nothing happened and wait for her to get over it. She always does.

The correct answer is number 1. If you really value someone's friendship, you need to make sure she

knows it. Being too stubborn to talk things over isn't going to help your friendship at all.

Pssst? Wanna know the secret of lasting friendship? Just remember the basic rule of manners — show respect for your friend and be kind. Having friends takes effort, patience, and time. Some friendships last a lifetime. Others are over before you know it. But every friendship has a better chance of lasting if you treat your friends exactly how you wish they would treat you.

How do you want to be treated? Have you ever given it any thought? Try making a list of the positive traits that you admire most in your friends. Ask yourself, "What are the qualities I think it's important for a friend to have?" List them below.

A Good Friend Is . . .

(Hint: How about supportive, reliable, able to compromise?)

_____

_____

_____

_____

_____

_____

_____

_____

_____

And while you're thinking about what good friends do, how about thinking about what they shouldn't do? List those friendship no-nos below.

A Good Friend Shouldn't . . .

(Clues: How about lie, talk about a friend behind her back, be jealous?)

_____

_____

_____

_____

_____

_____

_____

_____

_____

Putting these friendship dos and don'ts into practice can help to put your friendships on track. Remember the old saying, "The only way to have a friend is to be one"? It's really true. So treat your friends like the special people they are, and watch your friendships grow.

25

Social Sitches

Friendships put you in all sorts of situations in which it's important to know the right things to do. Grown-ups aren't the only ones who will be impressed by your manners. Your friends will be, too. Here are some pal pointers to help you through:

Pal Pointer #1: Be a Good Guest

If you're invited to your friend's home, your manners are gonna be on display not only to your friend but to her entire family.

Don't be a flake. The first thing you need to do is check with your parents to make sure the date and time are A-OK. If you don't want to go, don't say you will. But, once you confirm that you're going, don't cancel out at the last minute or show up an hour late. Being reliable is a good way to show your social savvy.

Be prompt and polite. As soon as you arrive, you'll want to greet your friend and her parents. If they don't answer the door right away, be patient. Nobody responds well to someone banging loudly on their door, so don't do it! Once they answer, make sure you greet them pleasantly. If you don't know her parents, and your friend doesn't introduce you, go ahead and introduce yourself.

Be the best guest ever. When you're at someone else's house, treat everything with care. Help to clean up anything you mess up, and make sure you don't complain about what your friend and her family have planned.

Don't raid the fridge without permission. If you're hungry or thirsty, ask politely if you can have a snack or a drink. Ask, too, if you may use the phone or the bathroom. Remember, you're a guest. Don't feel *too* at home!

Pal Pointer #2: When It's Time to Leave

Be prepared. First of all, make sure your parents know what time you're to be picked up. If you need to call them, ask permission to use the phone. Don't overstay your welcome. It's a manners misdemeanor to hang around waiting to be asked to stay for dinner or spend the night.

A few minutes before you're going to leave, gather your stuff together and put everything by the door. Then make sure you thank your friend and her parents for having you over.

Pal Pointer #3: Sleepover Strategies

If you've been invited to a sleepover, remember to bring your jammies, pillow, toothbrush, sleeping bag, and any toiletries you'll need. If your friend has a dad or brother living in the house, make sure your sleepwear is something you'll be comfortable wearing around him — or plan to stay dressed until it's time to go to bed.

Don't stay up all night giggling, screaming, and having fun. When her parents say "lights out," that's your cue to quiet down.

Pick up after yourself. Make sure you roll up your sleeping bag or make your bed. Don't leave anything behind.

Pal Pointer #4: When You're a Weekend Guest

If you're someone's guest for a weekend (or she takes you with her family on vacation), it's proper to bring a gift with you when you arrive. Something homemade (like a couple dozen chocolate-chip cookies) is always a nice gift.

Make them extra-special by wrapping them in a pretty tin or putting them on a decorative plate. **MM**[*]

Try to fit in. If you're staying with someone's family, it's really important that you adapt to their schedule. Eat *when* they eat, and eat *what* they eat. If your friend goes to bed at 11 P.M., don't stay up till 1 A.M. watching TV. If they've arranged a day at the beach, don't tell them you'd rather sit by the pool.

Ask permission before you do anything. If you want to take a shower, ask when it would be OK. If you need a towel, ask where you might find one. It's also a good idea to make sure you don't take too long in the shower and that you clean up the bathroom when you're finished.

At the end of the weekend, see if your friend's mom wants you to strip the bed. If the answer is yes, find out where to put the sheets and the blanket that you've used.

Within a week, send your friend's parents a thank-you note. (Check out the how-tos in Chapter 12.)

Pal Pointer #5: How to Score with the 'Rents

Guess what? Parents don't like rudeness. They don't like it when their own kids are rude, and they REALLY don't like it when other kids are. When you're a guest in a friend's home, it's important to put your best manners forward.

Try to get to know your friend's folks. Parents like to be talked to. You might bring up something about school to her mom, or talk to her dad about your athletic team. Always have a little bit of money with you. If everyone decides to go out for ice cream or to a movie, her parents will appreciate it if you *offer* to pay your way. If they insist on paying, that's fine, but be sure to thank them.

Do what you can to avoid bickering and fighting with your friend. Her mom and dad won't want to referee.

Pal Pointer #6: How to Be a Good Hostess

If you've invited someone to your home, it's up to you to make sure your friend has a good time. Figure out what you're going to do ahead of time, and if you can't agree on something, plan a compromise. When someone is your guest, her preferences should come first.

Make sure you don't ignore your guest. Don't decide you want to watch a video that she's not interested in, and don't get involved in a long phone conversation with another friend.

Try hard not to fight with your sibs or your parents when you've got a friend over. If your friend is staying for dinner, try to get her involved in your family's conversation.

When your friend is ready to leave, thank her for coming and see her to the door.

Friends Forever

Show your friends how much you care by practicing the three C's — Consideration, Commitment, and Compromise. Every good friend deserves the very best you can give her — not just on special days, but every day. Here's how the three C's work.

Consideration means that you go out of your way to think about someone else's feelings — you go that extra mile for someone you care about. You're willing to put your friend first — not necessarily all the time, but enough of the time to make her feel important. Considerate friends make others feel good. And they always try to see someone else's point of view. Allowing a friend to be herself and still liking her is a true act of friendship. Considerate friends are trustworthy, too. You'd hate to have your confidence betrayed, wouldn't you? Don't your friends deserve as much from you?

Commitment means that you know you're in the friendship for the long haul — not till a more popular friend comes along. Ditto, you won't flake on plans the minute something better comes up. Committed friends are willing to work on their relationship and put real effort into making it last. If you're not committed to working on your friendships, you'll probably find your buds are bailing on you. And who could blame them? Make sure your amigas know they can depend on you. Spend time helping a pal in need. Be there the next time your friend really needs to talk. You'll find that once friends know they can count on you, they'll value you for the good friend you are.

Compromise means that in some situations you'll get your way — and in others you won't. It's about give-and-take. It may be that you'll have to give up something you really want to do from time to time. But the payoff will be that because you're willing to compromise, your friends will be, too. You'll fight less, and you'll have more fun. Isn't that worth it?

MANNERS MELTDOWN

"My friend invited me to spend the weekend at her family's mountain cabin. I didn't know whether I should have brought a gift for her parents or not." — Caitlyn, age 11
Should Caitlyn have brought a gift? Would you? Find the **MM** * in this chapter and you'll have your answer.

33

Chapter 4:

Table Manners 101

What Would You Do?

Do your table manners need a makeover? Take the test below to see if your mealtime moves make the grade. Circle yes or no for each.

1. Salt and pepper shakers should be passed together. Yes No

2. It's considered polite to clean every bit of food off your plate. Yes No

3. When eating spaghetti, you should tuck your napkin into your shirt like a bib so that you don't drip sauce on yourself. Yes No

4. If you don't have a butter knife placed across your bread plate, it is proper to use your dinner knife to butter your bread. Yes No

5. Spoon your soup toward you so you can get it to your mouth more easily. Yes No

6. Always break your bread into pieces before you butter it. Yes No

7. Once you've used a knife, you should wipe it off with your napkin and place it back on the table. Yes No

8. The correct direction in which to pass food is to the person to your right. Yes No

9. When you've finished eating, make sure to drape (not fold) your napkin on the table to the side of your dinner plate. Yes No

10. If french fries are served with a main course that requires a knife and fork, it is still considered proper to eat them with your fingers. Yes No

Give yourself one point for each right answer. Correct answers: 1.) yes, 2.) no, 3.) no, 4.) yes, 5.) no, 6.) yes, 7.) no, 8.) yes, 9.) yes, 10.) no. If you scored 6 or better: You probably don't make too many table manners mistakes. But, read on. You'll definitely learn some new dining dos and don'ts.

If you scored 5 or less: You may be a little mixed up concerning your table manners. What to do? Study up and get the dish on manners maneuvers. Then be sure to practice, practice, practice.

When you sit down to eat, your manners are always showing. Knowing table manners can help you enjoy eating with others without worrying about making a mistake — or a mess. The following are some table tips to help get you through any meal.

Know Your Place Settings

Looking at everything set on a table can be confusing. You might wonder, "What do I do with all this stuff?" By following these easy rules, you'll be able to tackle even the toughest table.

Here's the silverware that you'll likely find at your place: two forks, a knife, and one or two spoons.

✳ The forks are placed to the left of the dinner plate. The salad fork is the smaller fork and is to the left of the regular fork.

✳ The knife is placed to the right of the plate with the cutting edge turned in toward the plate.

✳ The spoons are to the right of the knife.

Note: Fancier, more formal place settings may include special silverware for special courses — like smaller fish knives and forks to use with a fish course. A dessert fork or spoon might be set above your dinner plate or brought to the table with dessert.

User's Manual

After you've used a piece of silverware, you should rest it on your plate — don't put it back on the table. After using a knife, place it across the upper right-hand edge of your plate with the handle to the right and the blade resting on the plate. When you are completely finished eating, rest your fork and knife across the lower right-hand portion of your plate at about the four o'clock position.

The fork should be the closest to the bottom of the plate, prongs down, and the cutting edge of the knife blade should face toward you.

An easy rule: When you don't know which utensil to use, remember to work your way from the outside in. This means that the silverware that should be used for the food being served first will be placed the farthest away from your plate. Because soup and salad are usually served first, those forks and spoons are placed the farthest to the outside of your table setting. Still not sure which utensil to use? Watch your hostess for a clue and follow what she does.

These are the dishes you will probably find at your place: a dinner plate, bread-and-butter plate, salad plate, and glassware.

❋ The salad plate is to the left of the dinner plate.
❋ The bread and butter plate is at the top of the dinner plate, right above the forks.
❋ Your drinking glass is to the top right of the dinner plate.
❋ To the left of the entire setting is a folded napkin.

Tip: One of the best ways to become familiar with what goes where (and what it's for) is to help set the table!

Napkin Know-how

When you sit down at the table, the first thing you should do is open your napkin halfway and place it in your lap. The only exception: If a prayer is to be said before the meal, wait to place your napkin until after the blessing.

If you need to excuse yourself during the meal, place your napkin on your chair — not back on the table.

When you've finished eating, place the napkin loosely on the table, to the right of your plate. Don't fold it back the way it started.

Chow-how

Some foods are more difficult to eat than others. Here's the lowdown on chow-down challenges:

- **Soup** should be eaten by tipping the spoon slightly away from you and moving it toward the back of the soup bowl, then around to your mouth. Sound silly? There's a good reason for it: It helps you avoid sloppy spills on the table. If your soup is served in a large bowl, it's OK to leave your spoon in it when you're through. If it's served in a small bowl or a cup, place your spoon on the serving plate under it when you're through. Don't crumble your crackers into your soup. If you're served tiny oyster crackers, place them on your bread plate and add them to the soup two at a time.
- **Salad** that's served on a salad plate can be cut up with a knife and/or a fork. Because most table settings won't include a salad knife, go ahead and use your dinner knife. Don't stuff oversize salad into your mouth.

Just cut up a few bites at a time. If there's something you don't like, don't pick it out — just leave it on the plate uneaten. When you're through, place the knife you've used on the side of your salad plate. Remember this table manners tip: You don't want to use a knife to cut ANYTHING that's served in a bowl.

- **Fish (with bones)** must be eaten carefully so you don't swallow any of the bones. If, while you're chewing, you discover a little piece of bone in your mouth, work it toward the front of your mouth with your tongue, then discreetly push it out onto your fork and put it on the side of your plate. This works great for cherry pits, too.

- **Chicken or meat (with bones)** aren't hard to eat once you know the how-tos. Cut off as much meat as you can — one bite at a time. What you can't cut should remain uneaten. Remember, whether your meat has bones or not, slow and steady is the way to go. Don't cut up your entire portion at once.

- **Pasta** isn't as tricky as it seems. Spaghetti or fettucini (or any other long pasta) should be rolled, a couple of strands at a time, onto your fork. If you need to, use a spoon or the side of the dish for support. Bite off the ends if there are any stragglers left dangling.

- **Lemon wedges** should be pierced gently with the prongs of your fork before squeezing their juice onto fish, veggies, or into a glass of iced tea. That way, you create tiny holes for the juice to flow through. Make sure you cup your hand around the lemon wedge as you squeeze it so that you don't squirt juice into anyone's face (including your own!).

- **Finger foods** like pizza, ribs, or sandwiches can be eaten with your hands. French fries require special handling at times. They can be eaten with your fingers unless they're part of a meal where a fork's being used — like when you're having steak and fries! Then you should cut them into pieces and eat them with a fork. If you're ever in doubt about what to do, it's always a smart move to use a knife and fork.

Food Foul-ups

✳ If you don't like what's being served, there's no need to announce it. Just take a small portion of the dish you don't like and put it on your plate. Then take a couple of small bites.

Eat larger portions of the food you find appealing. That way, your hostess may not even notice that there's something you don't like. If you're a vegetarian or you're allergic to something that's being served, speak up. But, do it politely. It's OK to tell your hostess that you don't eat meat — or that you can't eat tomatoes because you're allergic to them.

❋ Never reach across someone to serve yourself. Unless something is easily within your reach, ask the person closest to you to pass it.

❋ Don't take huge bites. A bite-size portion of food should always be small enough to fit comfortably in your mouth.

❋ If you spill something, try to clean it up by dabbing a little water on it with your napkin. If it doesn't need immediate attention, just wait until the meal is over and then tell your hostess about it. Apologize and offer to help clean it up.

Table Manners Dos and Don'ts

Do wait for others to be served before you start eating.
Don't talk with your mouth full of food.

Don't leave your spoon in a coffee- or teacup. Rest it on your saucer instead.

Do bring the food to your mouth, not your mouth down to your plate.

Don't say things like "I'm so stuffed, I think I'm gonna explode," or "Oh, gross, I can't stand mushrooms!"

Don't use your fingers to push your food onto your fork or spoon. Use a slice of bread if necessary.

Don't blow on your food to cool it down.

Don't push your plate away when you're finished eating.

Do turn your head away from the table if you need to sneeze or cough.

Do say "Excuse me" if you need to get up during the meal.

Don't tilt back in your chair.

Don't ask for seconds unless you're sure there's enough for everyone.

Don't rest your elbows on the table.

Do thank your hostess for the nice meal.

Do come to the table when you're called and be sure to show up with clean hands.

Don't eat with your elbows sticking out. Keep them in toward your body instead.

Do use a finger bowl if one is presented.

It's a small bowl, half filled with water, that may be brought to the table during a formal meal. To use it, dip your fingertips in, one hand at a time, then dry with your napkin. **Do** put pits, seeds, celery ribs, or any other inedibles on your butter plate or on the edge of your dinner plate, not anywhere else.

Don't just jump up from the table when you're through eating. At home ask, "May I be excused?" At a friend's, wait until your friend asks to leave the table. Then do the same. In both cases, clear your own plates and take them into the kitchen.

Chapter 5:

Restaurant Rules

What Would You Do?

You've been waiting for the server to notice you for about ten minutes. To get his attention you decide to:

1. hold up your menu so that he knows you want his attention.

2. yell "Waiter!" at him the next time he's within shouting distance.

3. make eye contact with him when you see him walk by. Then raise your hand and say, "Excuse me. We're ready to order, please."

The right answer is number 3. Sometimes waiters and waitresses are really busy, and it's important to remind them politely that you are in need of their attention.

Whether you're headed out for a fast Big Mac or to somewhere nicer for a full-course meal, you'll want to know all about dining out.

Upon arriving at a restaurant, the first thing to do is check out the seating situation. If there's a host or hostess, that person will let you know when and where to be seated — and will show you to your table. Here's a term you may not know: *maître d'* (pronounced *maytra dee*). That's who does the seating in a nicer, more formal restaurant. If you look around and there's nobody to seat you, find an empty table and seat yourself. After you're seated, you shouldn't have to wait too long for your server to notice you and come to your table.

Menu Matters

You will be handed menus either by the hostess or the server, or you'll find them on the table. Either way, try to decide what you want to eat fairly quickly so that you're ready to place your order when the server comes to the table. If there's something on the menu that you don't understand, it's fine to ask for an explanation.

There are two ways to order from a menu, and you'll need to know the difference if you want to eat smart. *À la carte* means you pay for each item separately. The price will be listed next to the item on the menu. *Table d'hôte* (complete dinner) or *prix fixe* (fixed price) means you are charged a single price for a complete meal. The menu should tell you what's included.

If you are uncertain about what foods or side dishes come with your meal, it's OK to ask. Sometimes specials are not noted on the menu, so your server will offer to tell you about them. If you've already decided what you're having, it's fine to say, "Thank you, but we already know what we want." If you want to hear the specials and you decide to order one, it's a good idea to ask what the price is (if the server doesn't volunteer it).

Dining Dictionary

If there's a word you're not familiar with, don't be embarrassed to say so. It's better to ask what a marinara (tomato) sauce is than to find out later that you've ordered something you hate. OK, so here are some other words you may see on a menu and not have a clue what they mean.

Alfredo — a cream sauce that is
   frequently served over pasta
au gratin — with cheese

beurre — French for butter

boeuf — French for beef

brochette — on a skewer

bruschetta — grilled bread with a combination of tomatoes, garlic, and olive oil, usually served as an appetizer

calamari — squid

crème brûlée — a custardlike dessert with a carmelized sugar topping

en croûte — in a crust

filet — without bones

flan — a type of custard

gnocchi — potato dumplings that are usually served in Italian restaurants

pomme frites — French for fried potatoes (french fries)

huevos — Spanish for eggs

linguini — a type of thin spaghetti

penne — a type of pasta, a thin macaroni tube shaped like a pen quill

sorbet — a frozen ice, like sherbet

soup du jour — the soup of the day

vinaigrette — an oil-and-vinegar dressing

Food for Thought

During your meal, you'll want to be sure that you don't make any embarrassing manners mistakes.

Here are five easy-to-remember dos and don'ts.

1. **Don't** call attention to yourself or your group. Keep your voices down. Don't act silly, throw food, or make a big mess. If you and your friends have been given permission to go out without your parents, you should act mature.

2. **Don't** stare at the food someone else has ordered at another table. If something interests you, ask your server what it is.

3. **Do** send back your food if it's not served the way you ordered it or there's something wrong with it. Just be sure that you're polite about it. Say something like, "I ordered the sandwich on whole wheat and it's on rye. Would you please take it back and get me another one?" It's also OK to ask the waiter to replace dirty silverware, plates, or glasses.

4. **Don't** linger at the table too long after you've finished your meal — especially if you know that others are waiting for the table.

5. **Do** make sure you say "please" and "thank you" to your server. Even if the service is slow, you don't want to be rude in a restaurant — or anywhere else for that matter!

Check, Please!

Shortly after you've finished eating, the server should bring your check to the table. If you've waited a while (say, five minutes or more) and your check hasn't arrived, it's OK to ask for it.

As soon as you have the check, look it over to be sure you've been charged the correct amount and that your friends know how much they owe. A great way to avoid confusion is to ask for separate checks, but lots of restaurants don't like to do this, so you'll need to know how to figure out your share.

Your check will say whether you are to pay your server or the cashier. If it says to pay the cashier, make sure you have everyone's money before you go up to the cash register.

Most states charge tax on food bills, which can add 6 to 9 percent extra to your total. That means, if your tab totals eight dollars, you will owe an additional 45 to 65 cents for tax. If you're eating with three of your friends and nobody figures in the tax, you're going to be a couple of dollars short when you pay the bill.

Tips on Tipping

In most restaurants, a tip of about 15 percent of the bill (before the tax is added) is expected. In really expensive restaurants, that amount usually GROWS to 20 percent.

Here's how to do the math:

If your total is eight dollars (before tax), figure out what 10 percent of that amount is, then add half of that amount to the first total.

Example: 10% of $8 = 80 cents. 5% of $8 or half of 80 cents = 40 cents.

80 cents (10%) + 40 cents (5%) = $1.20 (15%). That is what your tip should be.

But what happens if the service is really bad? In that case, you can leave a reduced amount for a tip — say 10 percent. But, listen up! For the most part, unless the service is just horrible, you'll want to leave the customary tip. Not leaving a tip at all — or leaving only pennies — is not the right thing to do. * And if the food is bad, remember your server didn't cook it — she just brought it to you!

When You're Someone's Guest

You've probably been to an upscale restaurant with your family, and if so, your parents probably helped you out by telling you how to act. But when you're invited out by a friend's family, you'll need some extra dining-out know-how.

OK, so what do you do? First of all, when you're someone's guest, it's better to wait to see what she's going to order before making up your mind about what you're going to eat. Ask your friend and her parents what they're having. Their answers will help you decide on your own selection. You shouldn't order anything that costs *more* than what your friend has ordered.

When it comes to drinks, appetizers, salads, or

desserts, you should also wait to see what your host or hostess does. And be careful about asking for soft drink refills. Most nice restaurants charge for each and every refill.

Finally, when you've finished eating, you'll score politeness pointers by saying that your food was fine — even if it wasn't. Always avoid hurtful honesty — like telling someone's parents, "My steak was so tough I could hardly chew it." Offer a convincing thank-you — no matter what!

MANNERS MELTDOWN

"I was at a restaurant with my friends and we didn't get served for a long time. We didn't know whether to leave a small tip — or if that would be mean." — Sara, age 12

Could you come up with the answer to this on your own? Not to worry. Look for the **MM** * symbol in Chapter 5 — and you'll know what to do if it ever happens to you.

Chapter 6:

Say Hello to Good Phone Manners

What Would You Do?

Your parents are away for the night and the phone rings. The person says it's important that he speaks to your parents right away. You should say:

1. *"I'm sorry, they're gone until tomorrow. Please give me your name and number, and I'll have them call you back."*

2. *"They aren't available right now, but I'll have them return the call as soon as they can. May I have your name and number?"*

3. *"They aren't here. Can you call them back tomorrow?"*

The answer is number 2. When you're home alone, don't give out information about where

your parents are or when they're returning un-less you are sure you know who the caller is.

Whether you talk on the phone nonstop or you're more of the silent type, you'll want to check out the four-one-one on how to make better connections. Even though the person you're talking to can't see you, how you act on the phone can say a lot about the kind of person you are. Knowing how to answer the phone, how to take messages, and what to say in all kinds of situations are all part of doing the right thing. Want to know more? It's your call!

The Family Phone

Do you share a phone with your parents or your siblings? You probably do. And if you do, you probably know how problems with the phone can cause big family fights that make everybody really mad — or really moody. Why not have a talk with your family before the next battle breaks out? See if you can all come up with some telephone tactics that will help keep the peace. You can set rules for time limits, agree on how you'll answer the phone, and talk about taking messages. A few minutes of conversation now may save you from hours of arguments later on.

Dial M for Manners

Here are some basic phone rules whether you're answering the phone or dialing out.

* Don't be a phone hog. Be considerate and limit the length of your calls. Don't tell your siblings you'll be off in a minute and then keep them waiting for hours. Even if you don't share a phone, don't spend hours talking at the expense of studies, chores, and so on.
* Try to answer the phone with a friendly hello or in the way your parents have instructed you, even if you're busy doing something. If the phone is for someone else in the family, politely say, "Just a minute, please. I'll get her." Don't just stand there and scream the name into the phone!
* If you have call-waiting and it beeps, excuse yourself from the call, then see who's on the line. If the call is for another family member, finish your own call quickly and then call the person to the phone. Don't tell the new caller that you're on the phone so they'll have to

call back. If the second call is for you, tell them you'll get back to them. Then return to your original conversation. TIP: Make sure you do remember to call your friend back.

* If you're home alone, don't give any caller personal information — unless you know for sure who the person is. And don't ever let strangers know that your parents aren't home. Just say, "They're not available right now. If you want to leave your name and number, I'll have them call you back."

* Sound friendly. Someone's impression of what you're saying is going to be based on your tone of voice, and people usually respond positively to politeness.

* Speak clearly. Don't chew food or gum while you're talking to someone.

* If someone calls you at a bad time, tell them politely that you're busy and ask if you can call them back.

* Don't call people at improper times — meaning dinnertime, too late at night, or too early in the morning. It never hurts to ask someone if it's a good time to talk.

* If you're not sure who's on the line, it's fine to ask, "Who is this?"
* If you call someone, ask for her politely. If she isn't home, don't say, "Where is she?" Do say, "May I leave a message, please?" or "Would you please ask her to call _____?"
* If a friend's parent answers the phone, it's nice to say hello to them and to identify yourself. It's OK to say, "Hi, this is Trisha. Is Megan there?" It's even better to say, "Hi, Mrs._____. This is Trisha, may I speak to Megan, please?"
* If the phone rings six times and nobody answers, hang up and try again later.

Wrong Numbers

If you think you've dialed the wrong number, ask, "Is this 222-2222?" If it's not, say, "I'm sorry, I dialed the wrong number." Don't just hang up the phone.

If someone calls you and it's a wrong number, don't be rude. Just ask, "What number are you calling?" Don't give your number. If the number the caller wanted is yours, you might say, "That is our number, but there's no one here by that name."

Taking a Message

The Handwritten Kind

When you answer a call for someone who's not home, it's always a good idea to take a message. That means you have to have a pencil and paper by the phone so you don't have to go rummaging through the house while the caller is waiting. Always verify the caller's name and read back all phone numbers to be sure that you've gotten everything right. Here's the tricky part: After you take it, you have to make sure you deliver it.

Hopefully, if you take messages for the people in your family, they'll return the favor by taking messages for you!

Answering Machine Messages

Answering machines have sure made communicating easier, and most people can't imagine how they ever lived before the beep. When an answering machine picks up your calls, what do people hear? Is it something you'd want to listen to? Give some thought to what your outgoing answering machine message will sound like *before* you record it.

First, write down what you're gonna say and practice it a couple of times. Make sure that you sound friendly. Keep your message brief. If you're recording a message for the whole family, check with your parents to be sure they approve of what you're going to say.

If you play the machine's messages back when you get home, it's your job to write down everyone's messages. Agree on a good place to post everyone's messages.

When you leave a message on someone else's machine, be brief. Give only the important details. Don't go on and on for so long that you take up their whole tape.

Pagers

It's common for parents to have pagers. Maybe you or some of your friends do, too.

Here are some pager pointers you might want to follow:

✸ If you page your mom or dad, stay at a number where they can reach you.

- ✷ Don't page them for every little thing. Discuss with them when they think it's appropriate for you to page them — and when it can wait.
- ✷ Take your pager with you only when it's appropriate. Pagers should be turned off at school, at churches or synagogues, at movies, or anywhere they can cause a disruption.
- ✷ Give only your closest friends your pager number. Don't leave it on your answering machine.
- ✷ If someone pages you, return the page promptly.
- ✷ Tell your friends to page you only when it's important. Make sure you do the same with them.
- ✷ If you tell someone to page you, make sure you take your pager with you.

Calling Your Parents at Work

It's not a good idea to call your parents at work constantly. Frequent interruptions can be distracting on a normal day and downright disruptive on a busy one. For the most part, make sure you have a good reason to call. You can ask your mom or dad to give you some guidelines on when it's OK for you to call and when it's not.

If someone else answers your parent's work phone, be polite and pleasant. Make sure you identify yourself to whomever answers the phone. You might say, "Hello, this is Alison Watson. May I speak to Earl Watson, please?"

If your parent isn't in or isn't available, don't just hang up. Leave a brief, to-the-point message. Thank the message-taker politely.

If your parent is in, keep your conversation brief. It's a good idea to ask, "Do you have a few minutes to talk?" That way, if they're really busy, they can tell you.

Should Girls Call Boys?

Here's a sitch where what was once a big no-no is OK today. But you need to know some boy-calling basics:

It's OK When:

you have a legitimate question about schoolwork.
you're returning his call.
you are inviting him somewhere.

your mom or dad knows you're calling and
thinks it's OK.

It's Not OK When:

you just call to hear his voice and then
quickly hang up.
you're playing a prank.
you call over and over again.
you call for no reason.

Don't Call Us . . .

Obscene Phone Calls — They happen to everyone. Someone calls and says something mean,
scary, or inappropriate. If you receive a call like
this, hang up and tell your parents immediately.
Don't have a conversation with someone you
don't know. Don't stay on the line out of curios-
ity about what the person's going to say next.
Don't give out any information.

If the calls persist, you'll want to keep a
record. Your parents can contact the phone
company to see what else can be done. If you
have an answering machine, your parents may
want to screen your calls for a while. Or perhaps

they will ask *you* not to answer the phone for a short time.

Telemarketers — Callers trying to sell something can be a real pain. You might be tempted to just hang up on them, but it's better to be polite and try to cut the call short. Never give out any information about anyone in your family, no matter what the caller tells you. If you are certain that your parents won't want to speak with them, in your firmest voice simply say, "I'm sorry, we're not interested." If you get a lot of these calls, it's a good idea to ask your parents how they want you to handle them.

Chapter 7:

School Etiquette

What Would You Do?

Your teacher just asked everyone to hand in last night's homework assignment. The minute she asks for it, you remember that you left it on your desk at home. You should:

1. run up immediately and tell her that you left it home. Then beg her to let you go to the office to call your mom to see if she'll bring it to school.

2. think up an excuse that she's bound to understand — like that your electricity was out all night and you couldn't do the assignment in the dark. How can she argue with that?

3. wait until after class and then talk to your teacher. Tell her you did the assignment, but you left home without it. Apologize and ask if you can have your parent verify that

66

it was done, then turn it in a day late for partial credit.

The correct answer is number 3. Your teacher will appreciate your owning up to your mistake.

School is a great place to learn about all kinds of things — including how to act with your teacher, your friends, and other students.

Teacher Tactics

Treat your teachers with the same kind of respect you show your parents. During the hours you spend in the classroom, your teacher is in charge, just like your folks are when you're at home.

You may think your teacher is crabby, demanding, and unreasonable. But try smiling at her or saying hello, and see what happens. Everyone wins when people show common courtesy to one another.

During your years at school, you will have teachers you like and teachers you don't. One term you might feel like the teacher's pet, and the next year you'll swear the teacher hates you. You'll find that some teachers give more homework and harder tests. Some will love your creative writing, while others won't. Your job is to be well-mannered and to try your hardest — no matter what.

Here are some things you can do to make the grade at school:

* Pay attention in class. Do you like it when you're talking and someone ignores you? Nobody does — and that includes your teacher.
* Don't shout out the answer even if you're sure you're right. If you have something to say, raise your hand and wait to be called on.
* Do participate. You have a contribution to make.
* Don't disrupt the class by talking to your friends or passing notes. You'll do better in the course if you listen to what the teacher has to say.
* Don't cheat on tests, quizzes, or reports. Instead, study hard and do your own work. All that anyone expects from you is that you do your best.
* Make sure you write down all of your assignments and that you do a neat and careful job. Doing good work is something to strive for and be proud of.

※ Don't wait until you're failing the class to ask for help.

※ If you have a problem to discuss with your teacher, do it in private. Ask to see her before or after school, and tell her what's on your mind. It's not a good idea to have a private conversation with a teacher in front of the whole class.

Classmate Courtesy

During the school year you're going to be in social situations with lots of kids besides your friends. And guess what? You're not going to like everybody. But everyone deserves fair treatment — even those who are not your type.

If you forget all the other rules of manners, remember this one: ***Don't ever be mean to anyone.*** That means don't put people down so you can look cool. Don't make hurtful comments or try to embarrass kids in front of others.

Here are some other things you should think about:

※ If there's a new girl in your class, start a conversation with her. Ask her about an upcoming school activity or about her old school. Compliment her on her sweater or her hairstyle. Try to imagine how you would feel in her situation.

* If there's someone you really don't like, you don't have to hang out with her. Just remember, you don't have to be unkind or obvious about disliking her, either.

* If you and your friend are in a fight, don't tell the whole world about it. Don't try to get others in your group to take your side. Work it out with your friend one-on-one.

* Be friendly. Smile at kids who don't hang with your crowd. Talk to someone who looks as though she needs a friend.

During the school day, you'll want to make sure you show your respect for your school, too. How? It's easy. Don't litter. Don't throw gum or trash on the ground. Don't write on classroom walls, desks, or in the bathroom.

Lunchtime Lowdown

You're not gonna be graded on the way you act at lunch, but you should still practice good manners. Like not throwing food, being sure to pick up your own trash, and sharing your lunch with a friend who's left hers at home. And not mooching off everyone else all of the time.

If you're in the lunch line, make up your mind about what you're going to order before you get to the front. Don't keep everyone waiting while you decide between mac and cheese and a burger. And be sure to wait your turn. It's not cool to push your way to the front of the line even if your BFF is way up there.

Library Rules

You already know the most important library rule: SHHHHHH. That's right. Time spent in the library is quiet time. You'll want to keep your voice down and get something accomplished. Did you come to read a book or look up some information on the Internet? Get to it!

Make sure you take special care of any books you borrow. Don't write in them or rip out pages. Return them on time so that someone else can use them. If you look at books but don't check them out, make sure you put them back or return them to the librarian.

Remember, using the library is a privilege. Earn it and deserve it.

Chapter 8:

How to Make the Manners Team

What Would You Do?

Your soccer team has a game this weekend. You've just been invited to go with your friend to an amusement park and you really want to go. You should:

1. call your coach the night before the game and tell him you're sick.

2. talk to your coach ahead of time to see if he thinks it would be OK to miss this one game.

3. show up because you have to, but sit on the bench and sulk. After all, you'd rather be somewhere else.

The right answer is number 2. In a situation like this, it's the coach's call whether a player can miss a game or not. Team players know they've

gotta give the best they've got — 100 percent of the time. It's always a bad move to show up and play with a bad attitude.

No matter what sport you're playing, being an MVP means always remembering that courtesy counts. You'll score before, during, and after the game when you follow the rules of good sportsmanship. Here's the game plan.

Most Valuable Plays

Real winners know that it's their responsibility to show up on time. For games and for practices. It's important to the whole team that everyone's committed and serious. That means that every player has to have a good attitude.

Good sportsmanship starts with showing respect for teammates, coaches, and the other team. Only losers mope when they miss a ball, pout when things go wrong, or make fun of other players.

Even if you're faced with a call that seems unfair, you shouldn't mouth off to the person in charge. Being a good sport is always about playing the best game you know how and not complaining about an official's decisions.

73

When your team loses (and you will), you shouldn't act like it's the end of the world (it isn't). Congratulate the other team, and shake hands with each player after the game's over. You'll stand out if you're known as someone who can accept a loss and move on.

No matter how good a player you are, never think you're the most important person on the team. All team members contribute to the outcome of the game. Likewise, don't blame others when something goes wrong. Don't make excuses or dwell on your mistakes. And don't ever throw a tantrum — OR a piece of equipment.

Try to have a good relationship with your coach. Show respect for her opinions, and remember, a coach's role is to teach you how to improve your skills. You won't love every coach you have, but you will need to do your part to have a good relationship with each of them. If you need to talk about something (perhaps you have to miss the next game or you've hurt your wrist and can't pitch), arrive at practice a little early to see your coach when she's not trying to do a million other things. * You'll be surprised by how much more understanding she'll seem to be.

When You're a Spectator

Hey, sports fans. Be sure to check out these stadium standards.

* Arrive before the game starts so you're not trying to get to your seat during the national anthem or during the game. Stand for "The Star-Spangled Banner."
* Try not to block anyone's view, kick the seat of the person in front of you, or crowd your neighbor with your belongings. Don't talk so loudly that you disturb others. Go ahead and cheer for your favorite team, but it is not cool to boo the competition.
* If you have to go to the rest room or you want refreshments, try to do so during a break in the action. If you get something to eat, be careful not to spill it all over your neighbor. When the game's over, don't push anyone while you're trying to exit.

MANNERS MELTDOWN

"I twisted my ankle riding my bike and I had a soccer game that Saturday, but I couldn't run very well 'cause it still hurt. I didn't say anything, though, because the coach was kinda mean and I didn't want him to yell at me." — Morgan, age 10

OK, what would you tell Morgan to do? If you don't know, look back for the * in this chapter and find out.

Chapter 9:

Party Etiquette

What Would You Do?

Your friend bought you a birthday present and you really hate it. It's an ugly color, and you'd never, ever wear it. You should:

1. tell her about the gift Alexis gave you. Maybe she'll get a clue.

2. wait until her birthday and then try to find something really ugly to give to her.

3. thank her politely and find something nice to say about the gift.

The answer is number 3. Sometimes even friends don't know exactly what to give to another friend, but you should never compare one person's gift to another's — or make anyone feel bad about what she's given you.

Having a party? Headed for a party? Whether you're a hostess or a guest, there are plenty of party pointers you'll want to know.

If you're the hostess, make sure that you give a lot of thought to who you're going to ask and how you're going to do the inviting. You won't want to hand out your invitations at school unless you're going to be inviting everyone in your class. And if that's not your plan, it's best to do your inviting by phone, mail, or e-mail.

Be sure you and your buds play it cool at school when talking about the party plans. Sure, you're all excited. Who wouldn't be? But you don't want to mention your party in front of kids who aren't included. Why hurt someone else's feelings?

Make sure that your invitations contain all the party info anyone could possibly need to know. You'll want to tell everyone who's giving the party, the occasion, the date and time (be sure to give them a beginning and ending time), your address or the location of the party, the kind of dress that's appropriate, if they need to bring anything, and where to R.S.V.P.

R.S.V.P. means you want your guests to reply to let you know if they're coming. The word is short for a French phrase — *répondez s'il vous plaît* — meaning please reply. That way, you'll know how many kids you can expect. So be sure to include your phone number so they can let you know. Tip: It's also a good idea to put a date to reply by so that everyone doesn't call the day before the party to tell you if she's coming.

The Hostess To-do List

On the day of your party, here's a list of things you'll want to do to be a perfect hostess.

* Make sure you're ready about ten minutes early so that you can greet your early arrivals yourself.
* Show your guests where to put their belongings.
* If it's your birthday and a guest has brought you a gift, say thank you. If a guest hasn't brought a gift, don't say, "Where's my present?"
* If your guests don't know one another, introduce them. Be especially sure to introduce someone who doesn't know anyone else. **MM** *
* Spend time with all your guests, not just your best friends.
* When it's time to open presents, open them randomly. Don't promise your best friend that you'll open hers first.

* Say something nice about every gift, such as, "Wow, I love fruity bath gel! Thanks." Even if you hate it, say something like, "That was so nice of you. Thank you soooo much." Or, "Great color. I've been wanting something sea green."

* Don't make price comparisons about the gifts you receive. Sure, your best friend may spend more than someone you know from school. Don't say, "Wow, I can't believe how much you spent on my gift!"

* When you play games or serve food, remember that you're there to see that your friends have a good time, too. You're not necessarily supposed to win the prize or get the biggest piece of cake for yourself.

* When each of your friends leaves, stop what you're doing and walk her to the door. Tell her good-bye and thank her for coming and (if it applies) for the gift.

* When the party's over, help your parents clean up.

80

When You're the Guest

Everyone loves to be invited to parties. It's a great way to get together with your buds and to share lots of fun times and special occasions. One of the most important things a guest can bring to any party is good manners — and a great attitude. What else can you do to be the kind of guest who keeps being invited back? You can put these helpful party-perfect suggestions into practice.

❋ Be prompt. It's important to a party's hostess that the guests don't arrive too early or too late — but right on time.
❋ If you're invited to a birthday party (or another special occasion), you should bring a gift — unless you're told not to. Buy what you can afford, or see if someone else wants to go in on a gift with you. You don't have to blow a month's allowance trying to impress somebody. Don't try to "buy" friendships with overpriced gifts.
❋ Bring your smile to every party you attend. It's not OK to show up in a bad

mood or to bring your problems to the celebration.

* Even if you don't feel like it, join in and participate. Think the game everyone's playing is sorta lame? Be a good sport, and don't say a word about it.

* Be friendly to everyone — whether they're your friends or not.

* Be respectful of someone else's property. Don't race through the house or track in mud from outside.

* Even though you're there to have a good time, a good guest offers to help the hostess. See if you can pitch in to serve the cake or offer to pick up discarded gift wrapping.

* No matter how much fun you're having, leave on time — after thanking your hostess for inviting you.

A Slumber Party

If the party you're invited to is a sleepover, here are some ways to make sure you don't doze off in the courtesy department.

Bedtime Don'ts

Don't stay up all night long yelling, scream-ing, and giggling, especially after your friend's parents have issued a "quiet down" warning.

Don't leave the house unless the parents know about it.

Don't raid the refrigerator unless some-thing is offered to you.

Don't play mean tricks on someone who's fallen asleep early.

Don't wake up early and make a lot of noise.

Don't ask, "When's breakfast?" Wait to be invited to eat something.

Don't expect someone else to roll up your sleeping bag. Take care of your own things, and have them all together by the time your parents arrive to pick you up.

Also, when your parents drop you off, make sure you tell them what time you'll need them to pick you up the next day.

MANNERS MELTDOWN

"I was invited to a party and I didn't know anyone. I was hoping the hostess would introduce me to her friends, but she didn't. I didn't know what to do." — Olivia, age 9

Was it wrong of Olivia to expect the hostess to introduce her around? Find the **MM** * in this chapter, and you'll know what to do if this happens to you.

Chapter 10:

Computer Courtesy

What Would You Do?

You're online trying to research a science project and all of your cyber-buddies start sending you instant messages. You should:

1. *tell them you're working on schoolwork and you'll call them later.*

2. *totally ignore them. You're busy. They'll just have to wait.*

3. *answer them and then decide to forget the science project. Cyber-chatting with your friends is way more fun.*

The correct answer is number 1. How would you feel if your friends just ignored you? It's way better to let your buds know that you're doing something important than to let them wonder why you're not responding.

Computers are a totally cool way to keep in touch. But like everything else, there are lots of manners tips and how-tos that can help you make your way through cyberspace. And you won't find the instructions in your computer manual.

If you have your own computer, you're lucky. You don't have to worry about sharing computer time (and space) with others in your family. If you don't have access to a computer, you can log on at school or the library. There, you'll need to be extra careful to follow all of the rules. But if your computer is the family computer, here are some cyber-courtesies you'll definitely want to follow:

❋ If your parent or sibling wants to use the computer for something important (like doing bills or doing homework), your computer socializing will definitely have to wait. To avoid a hassle, your family should set up some computer guidelines that each of you agrees to follow.

❋ It's up to everyone to keep the space around the computer clean. That means you shouldn't eat or drink near your computer. And if you do, make sure you don't use the keyboard if your fingers are messy or sticky.

※ No way should you ever do any cyber-snooping. Other family members' computer files should be off limits to everyone else. Respect your family's privacy on the computer, just as you do everywhere else, and hopefully your parents and sibs will do the same for you.

Surfing Strategies

If you spend a lot of time online, you've got a fun, exciting world at your fingertips. Whether you're e-mailing a friend, responding to an instant message from a buddy, or visiting a chat room, you'll need some user-friendly advice. Bad manners in cyberspace can add up to a big manners malfunction — and some even bigger misunderstandings. Don't let it happen to you!

E-mail Etiquette

Before you e-mail your friends or anyone else, learn these cyber-strategies.

※ Always know who you're e-mailing and from whom you're receiving e-mails.
※ Think carefully about what you write or

forward. **MM** * Cyber-chat is easily misinterpreted. It can also be easily saved or printed out by another person.

* Be careful with anger, sarcasm, or humor. There are no verbal or visual clues to help a person interpret your message.
* Always use good taste and be respectful. Don't make up anything that isn't true. E-mail may seem harmless and unimportant, but it isn't.
* If you are e-mailing people regularly, be sure to check your e-mails, too.
* If you plan to e-mail someone frequently, make sure it's OK with her or her parents.
* Know the lingo. Don't type in all capital letters unless you're angry. Learn common computer abbreviations that others might use. Like BTW (by the way), GTG (got to go), LOL (laughing out loud), JK (just kidding), BRB (be right back). Use a :) as a sideways symbol for a smile.

Chatroom Courtesy

If you're in a chat room, there are certain good-behavior guidelines you'll want to follow.

* First of all, stay on the topic.
* Remember that you're voicing your opinion in a public forum.
* Don't put down someone else for having a different opinion.
* Try to make it clear when you are kidding and when you are serious.

Instant Messages

Do you have everyone you know on your buddy list? Are you on theirs? Cool deal. It's lots of fun to know when all your friends are on-line and to be able to communicate with them. To make sure that all of your communications transmit smoothly, here are some things you need to know:

* Instant messages arrive immediately. When someone sends you one, she is waiting for an answer pronto. If you're too busy doing something else, or you're already on-line with another group of friends, be sure to let your other bud know that you're not available to "chat."
* Remember, you're not on the phone. The person you're communicating with can't

even hear the tone of your voice. Think about what you write before you write it to avoid any misunderstandings or hurt feelings. You might want to read back what you've written before you hit the SEND button.

❋ Don't be a cyber-pest. If you don't get a response from someone, wait a few minutes and try again. Still don't get a response? Give it up and try again later. Don't keep buggin' your bud with messages like, "Well, I guess you're too good for me" or "Fine, go ahead and ignore me."

Cyber-safety

Make sure you surf safely by learning these tips:

❋ Don't share your password with anyone except your parents.

❋ Discuss with your parents when you can be on-line and where you can go on-line. Obey their rules.

❋ Never give out your real name or any personal information without your parents' permission.

- If anything weird or creepy comes to you by e-mail, make sure you tell your parents.
- Never get together with anyone you've "met" on-line. If someone asks to meet you in person, inform your mom or dad immediately.
- Be smart. If you think that something is a little strange, it probably is. Don't do anything risky.

MANNERS MELTDOWN

"I was on-line and my friend sent me an e-mail about another friend. I forwarded it to another friend, and the person who it was about was over at her house and read it. She got really mad at all of us, but I don't think it was my fault 'cause I wasn't the one who wrote it. I just forwarded it to show my friend." — Rachel, age 11

If you read this chapter carefully, you know what Rachel did wrong. If you missed it, look back and find the *.

Chapter 11:

Baby-sitting Behavior

What Would You Do?

You've got a baby-sitting job tonight, but you woke up this morning with a bad sore throat and you're feeling really crummy. You should:

1. *wait until the last minute to see if you're better. If you're not, then call and say you're sick and can't make it.*

2. *go anyhow and try not to breathe on the kids. People get really mad when sitters cancel at the last minute, and you don't want them to be mad at you.*

3. *call as early as possible. If you can, see if you can line up a friend to take your place.*

The correct answer is number 3. You should never baby-sit when you're sick. It's not fair to pass on those bugs to others. Besides, you probably wouldn't do your best job if you weren't

feeling well. If you do have to cancel, let the parents know as soon as possible, and see if you can find someone to fill in for you. Parents will really appreciate it if you tell them that you can't come, but you have a friend who can.

Are you ready to start baby-sitting? That's a question only you and your parents can answer. Some girls start sitting as early as 11 or 12. Others don't feel ready until they're 13 or 14. If you're already baby-sitting or will be allowed to soon, here are some tips to get you started.

A good way to try out your baby-sitting talents is to take care of someone else's kids while a parent is still at home. Doing this can help you to become familiar with the kids, the responsibilities, and the demands of the job with an adult standing by. Another way to test your baby-sitting skills is at home — by sitting for your younger brothers or sisters.

After you and your parents agree that you're old enough and responsible enough to start baby-sitting, you should think about taking a baby-sitting class. The American Red Cross offers classes all across the country. Or you can call your town's community center, park district, or local Y. They may offer classes as well. Taking a class will help you learn what you need to know to be a good baby-sitter. And parents will feel better about hiring you when they know you've taken the steps to become more sitter-savvy. Here's the scoop on being a first-rate baby-sitter.

Things to Do Before You Start

✳ Make sure you, your parents, or someone you know is acquainted with the family you're baby-sitting for.
✳ Let your parents know where you'll be and what the address and phone number are.
✳ When you accept a job, agree ahead of time how much you'll be paid. Write down all the job details: the parents' names and address, the date and time, their phone number, and what time they will pick you up (or what time they expect you to arrive).
✳ Don't cancel at the last minute unless it's an emergency.

On the Job

✳ Introduce yourself to the kids.
✳ Make sure the parents leave you a num-

ber where they can be reached, including their cell phone number, if they have one.

* Ask the parents if there are any special instructions you will need to follow.
* Don't invite friends over or use the phone unless you've asked permission.
* Make sure you lock all the doors once the parents leave.
* Don't raid the fridge without permission.
* Don't snoop.
* Once the kids are asleep, it's OK to watch TV, do homework, or read a book. Before that, the kids deserve your full attention.
* Know emergency numbers. You'll want the family doctor's number and the number of a neighbor who is home for the evening.

At the End of the Day

If you enjoyed the kids and want to sit again, let the parents know. Tell them, "I really loved watching your kids. I hope you'll call me again when you need a sitter." If they do call again and you can't sit, tell them, "Thanks for asking. I'd really love to, but I already have plans. I hope you'll try me again."

Chapter 12:

Mail Manners

What Would You Do?

You meant to write your friend's parents a thank-you note for the weekend you spent at their lake house. You kept putting it off for days, then weeks, and now it's been a whole month. Which answer do you think is correct? You should:

1. *forget about it. Thank-you notes need to be written within two weeks.*

2. *write a note anyhow. It's always better to write late than never.*

3. *call them. It's fine to write or call — and at least your call will reach them right away.*

The correct answer is number 2. Though a thank-you note should be written promptly, it is way better to write late than not to write at all. Calling to say thanks is a weak substitute for a written thank-you.

Special Delivery Tips

If your manners are in the mail, it's usually because you've written a thank-you note. It's easy to say thank you to someone for a gift or a kindness. But for some reason, it's hard to write. Why do you think that is? Maybe it's because you don't know what you should say, or you're not sure when a note is appropriate. This should help: If you're in doubt about whether or not you should send a thank-you, it's always better to go ahead and write one.

Here's another tip: You should always send a thank-you for any gift that is sent to you rather than delivered in person. That way, the person will know that you received it. Make note of these other rules about when and how to send thank-you notes.

Rule 1. It isn't necessary to send a thank-you for gifts you are given in person and for which you have already said thank you. Even so, it's nice to send a written expression of your appreciation.

Rule 2. Send a thank-you note to a friend's parents after you've been a weekend guest in their home. Even if you've already thanked them in person, you need to write them, too. Generally, thank-you notes are not necessary if you spend just one night with a friend. (Check this out with your mom and dad to see if they agree.)

Rule 3. Write the note promptly — within one week. Putting it off won't make it any easier, so just do it. Don't make your mom nag you to get it done. And don't think that if you wait long enough, you'll get out of it. You may lose points for lateness, but even a late thank-you is better than none.

Rule 4. Don't send a printed thank-you or something you typed on the computer. Your thank-you note should be written by hand. Personal stationery or cards that are blank inside are best. If you insist on using a printed card, make sure you add something personal.

Rule 5. Always mention something special about the gift. You might write about where you've worn it or how much you like the color. If you're acknowledging money, make sure you give the person some idea of what you're planning to buy with it. Be friendly and make your greeting personal. It doesn't have to be long, but it does have to sound sincere.

Rule 6. If you didn't really like the gift or it didn't fit, you don't need to mention that. Remember the saying, "It's the thought that counts." Well, that's true. So thank the gift giver even if the gift isn't to your liking. Find something nice to say — and say it. *

Rule 7. Reread what you've written and check your spelling before sending it. Still don't know what to say? Here are some suggestions:

If you stayed at someone's home, make sure you mention something you all did.

Example:

Dear Mr. and Mrs. Ryder,
    Thank you so much for letting me stay at your house this past weekend. I had the best time ever. It was so much fun baking cookies with Ali. I can't believe how many we ate! They were yummy.
    I hope we can take Ali with us somewhere soon. Thanks again for everything.

    Sincerely,

If your grandmother sends you money, be sure to tell her what you're going to buy with it.

Example:

Dear Gramma Jenny,

Thank you so much for the check you sent for my birthday. I'm going to use it to buy a new sweater that I've been wanting. I know I'll enjoy shopping for it.

I hope that you are feeling better and that I get to see you soon.

Thanks for always thinking of me.

Lots of love,

If you want to send a thank-you to a relative, bring them up-to-date on some of your family news.

Example:

Dear Aunt Joan,

I love the T-shirt you sent for my birthday. It fits great. I can't wait to wear it to my friend's party.

Mom and Dad have been really busy with work. They are planning to take us all skiing for the holidays, and I can hardly wait.

Thanks again for the thoughtful gift. I hope you are all fine.

Love,

If you decide you do want to send a thank-you note to a friend even though you've already thanked her in person, mention the gift in some way.

Example:

Dear Carlie,
I just love the cool PJs with the daisies all over them. They are sooooo cute. I wore them last night, and they're really comfy. You're the best.

I'm glad you could come to my party. I hope you had as much fun as I did.

Love ya lots,

Sealed with a Kiss

There are other reasons why you might want to send notes or cards to someone. When you are at camp or on vacation, friends and family will love to hear how you're doing. Don't know what to write? Think about what you would say to them if you were talking on the phone, then put it down on paper.

When it's someone's birthday, it's always nice to send a card. And sympathy notes and get-well cards tell someone you're thinking of them at a time when they really need to know that you care.

MANNERS MELTDOWN

"I got a gift from my parents' friends and I really didn't like it. I didn't know what to say about it in a thank-you note, so I wasn't sure whether to send one or not." — Laura, age 12

Do you think Laura should have sent a note? Bet you can find the answer by looking back through this chapter for the **MM** *.

Chapter 13:

Sticky Situations

Every now and then you may find yourself in a situation that will really test your social skills. Just remember, there's nothing you can't handle. Use your kindness and common sense, and you'll work your way through even the most challenging moments.

Here's some advice for mastering some of those tricky times.

"My friend and her family are from another country. Sometimes I'm not sure how to react to things when I'm over at her house, and I'm afraid I'll do or say something embarrassing."

Just be yourself and allow your friend and her family to be themselves, too. Our country's diversity presents new and exciting opportunities for everyone to learn more about other countries and other cultures. First of all, remember that the basic foundation of manners — respect for others — is something everyone understands and responds to.

Don't let anxiety about making a social blunder cause you to appear distant or unfriendly. Speak up, and ask your friend questions about things you don't understand. You'll find that friendliness and sincerity will get you through almost any social minefield. And your friend and her family will probably be willing to overlook (and perhaps laugh with you at) any innocent manners mishaps.

Sometimes someone else's customs can be confusing. Their food can be unfamiliar and even unappetizing. But true friendship knows no geographic boundaries. So share some of your family's traditions with them, and they'll probably welcome the opportunity to share theirs with you, too.

"My friend's pet died, and I don't know what to say to her."

It's not easy to deal with death. It's difficult to know what to do. And it's even more difficult to know what to say. The best thing you can do for your friend is just to be there.

Let her know that if she wants to talk, you've

got the time to listen. Encourage her to tell you about her feelings. Let her see that you recognize that she's sad and that you understand.

If she doesn't call you, give her a call. Make plans to do something you know she likes to do, and then include her. It takes time to get over a loss, but knowing that others care and support you really does help.

You might want to send your pal a note of sympathy, too. In your note you should acknowledge the death and let your friend know that you feel sad about it. Share something personal with her like, "I remember the time Fuzzy climbed up on the bed and ate all our popcorn!" Close your note by expressing your support and your sympathy.

"My friend's parents are getting a divorce, and she's acting really distant."

Let your friend know that you understand (even if you don't) and that you're there for her. If your own parents are divorced, this is a great opportunity for you to share some of your own experiences with her. Tell her how you felt, what you did to make yourself feel better, and finally, help her to see that you lived through it and you're doing fine.

If you can't relate to what she's going through, you can still be the most supportive friend around. Maybe you can help her connect with a friend you both have whose parents are divorced. It really does help to know that you're not the only one this has ever happened to.

Do your best to understand her mood swings, and do what you can to cheer her up when she's really feeling down. Make sure you tell her that she's got nothing to feel ashamed about. Encourage her to talk about how she's feeling and what she's thinking. It will really help her to express her feelings.

Invite her over to your house, and let her know that she's welcome anytime. Because she'll be feeling fragile for a while, be extra careful with her feelings.

"I was adopted and I don't know whether to tell people or not."

There's no reason to hide the fact that you were adopted. It's not something you should feel ashamed of in any way — in fact it's something that makes you who you are. If you don't know what to say to friends, ask your mom or dad. They can help you find the right words to use to explain how you and your parents became a family. It's also perfectly fine to simply say, "I was adopted," and leave it at that. If you feel OK about it, others will, too.

Conclusion

Congratulations! You've learned the lowdown on being respectful, courteous, and kind. In short, you've learned to treat the people in your life just the way you want them to treat you. You've also learned what to do in all kinds of social situations. You should now be prepared to head out and put into practice some of the manners you've discovered. Obviously, you won't remember every little tip and how-to you've read. But the more you do it, the easier it will get. And if you mind your manners often enough, you will begin to experience the magic of manners. Meaning, you'll feel so good about yourself that you'll find that others will respond better to you, too.

Good manners aren't just for today. They're for every day. What you've read in this book will make you feel cool, confident, and totally in control. So grab your manners, and take them with you everywhere you go. You know what to do! Now, go out and do the right thing!